Biography

The Author Peter Klessa Ramazani was born 1950 in Germany. 1979 he moved to Denmark. There Peter Klessa Ramazani worked among others as a cellar master and coffee roaster in a restaurant in Copenhagen and in the film and advertising industry. He was also trained as a massage therapist. Peter Klessa Ramazani lives frequently in Tuscany. 2013 he started to publish the eBook series "My Impressions of Italy". He also published the eBooks "Reflexology for everyone", "Reflexology learned quickly and easily", and "Massage your partner at home". His eBooks are published in English, German, Italian, Portuguese, Spanish, French, Japanese, some in Swedish and Dutch. 2015 he published the German novel "Blood Red Palms" and the historical documentary "Book of Terror".

Introduction

This book part 4 about the Herculaneum excavations takes you back to the year 79, where time has stood still there. From the entrance, I went systematically through the area with my cameras, and have selected more than 100 of the best images for you. I have taken all the photographs myself, and also have the copyright. Enjoy this walk through one of the best preserved excavation sites in Italy.

Some info about Herculaneum

The ancient city of Herculaneum, like Pompeii perished during the eruption of Vesuvius in 79AD. Although the city from pre-Roman times is not as well-known as Pompeii, but certainly no less interesting. The name suggests that the settlement was of Greek origin. At the time of the destruction by Vesuvius, Herculaneum had about 4,000 inhabitants. Herculaneum was so much smaller than Pompeii. In this small port city, trade did not matter too much. The trade was based mainly on fishing, agriculture and handicrafts. However, the features of the various excavated houses indicates partially great wealth of its inhabitants. Rich

Romans built their villas in Herculaneum and lived there together with slaves and artisans. The most famous villa is the Villa dei Papiri, because archeologists found a library of papyrus scrolls there. At the first outbreak of Vesuvius, Herculaneum was not as much affected as Pompeii. It has long been suspected that almost all the inhabitants managed to escape because there were very few skeletons in the excavated areas. As archeologists in 1982 expanded the excavation area on the ancient beach of Herculaneum, they made a surprising discovery. Inside of twelve boathouses were found huddled together about 250 skeletons. You can see pictures of it in the book. Herculaneum was completely buried under a volcanic layer of up to 20 meters, which later compressed to tuff.

My first view on Herculaneum.

The houses look surprisingly well preserved.

I will start just after the bridge and go up the street Cardo III Inferiore.

Casa di Aristide

In the courtyard of Casa di Aristide.

The house across the street.

Casa dello Scheletro

Casa dello Scheletro, House of the skeleton.

Casa dello Scheletro

Casa dello Scheletro

Casa dello Scheletro

Casa dello Scheletro

Thermopolium

Casa di Galba

Casa di Galba

Casa di Galba

Casa di Galba

Casa di Galba

Terme maschili

Terme maschili – Public bath form men.

Terme maschili.

Terme maschili.

Terme maschili.

Outside the bathhouse.

Casa di due otri, the house with the two gardens.

Casa di due otri

Sede degli augustali

Sede degli augustali, the house of the Augustus.

Sede degli augustali. To the right a painting showing Hercules.

Sede degli augustali. To the right a painting showing Hercules.

Sede degli augustali, well-preserved half-timbered.

Thermopolium

At the end of the street Cardo III Inferiore I go to the right.

At the street Cardo III Inferiore

At the street Cardo III Inferiore

Bottega ad cucumas, Workshop of Cucumas.

Casa del salone nero

Casa del salone nero, the house with the black salon. Charred entrance.

Casa del salone nero. The courtyard.

Casa del salone nero

Casa del salone nero

Casa del salone nero

Casa del salone nero. The black salon.

Casa del salone nero

Casa del salone nero. The black salon.

At the road IV Superiore.

Casa del bel cortile.

Casa del bel cortile. The house with the beautiful courtyard.

Casa del bel cortile. Again you see charred half timbered.

Casa del bel cortile

Casa del bel cortile. Stairs to the upper floor.

Casa del bel cortile

Casa del bel cortile

Casa del bel cortile

Casa di nettuno e anfitrite.

Casa di nettuno e anfitrite. The House of Neptune and Amphitrite.

Casa di nettuno e anfitrite

Casa di nettuno e anfitrite

Casa di nettuno e anfitrite

Casa di nettuno e anfitrite

Casa di nettuno e anfitrite

Terme femminili

Terme femminili – Public bath for women.

Terme femminili.

Terme femminili.

Terme femminili.

Terme femminili – Public bath for women.

Casa sannitica

Casa sannitica

Casa sannitica

Casa sannitica

Casa sannitica

Casa del tramezzo di legno.

Casa del tramezzo di legno. The house with the wooden wall.

Casa del tramezzo di legno

Casa del tramezzo di legno

Casa del tramezzo di legno

Casa del tramezzo di legno

Casa del tramezzo di legno

Casa del papiro dipinto. The house with the papyrus painting.

Casa della fullonica. The house of Fullonica.

Casa dell´alcova.

Casa dell´alcova. The house of the alcove.

Casa dell´alcova

Casa dell´alcova

Casa dell´erma di bronzo.

Casa dell'erma di bronzo. The house with the bronze figure.

Casa dell´erma di bronzo

A view up the well preserved street Cardo V Superiore.

The street Cardo V Superiore.

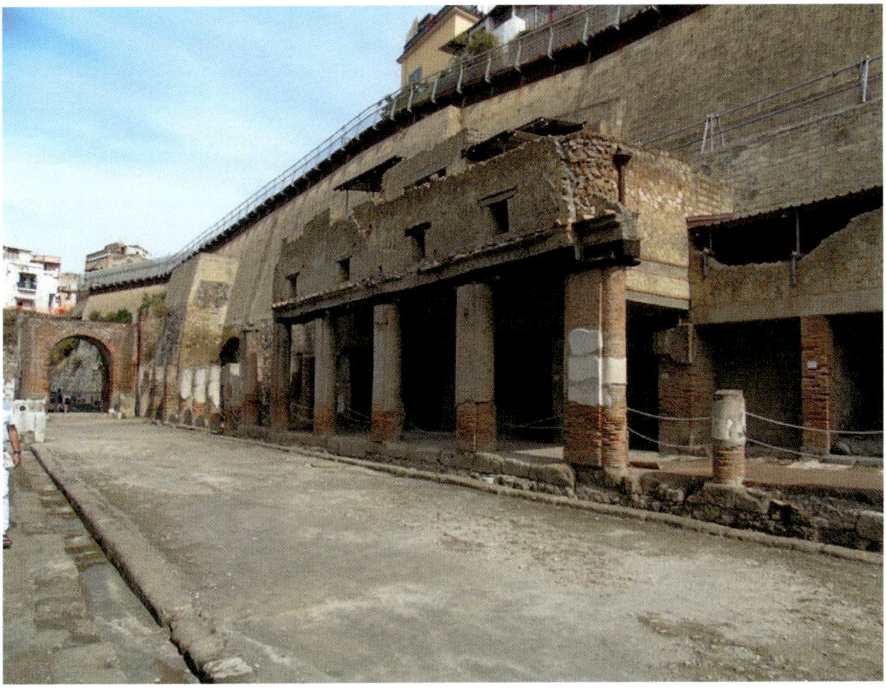

A house on the street Cardo V Superiore with two floors.

A view up the street Cardo V Superiore.

Pistrinum e bottega di sex patulcius Felix.

Pistrinum e bottega di sex patulcius Felix. Sex Shop of Patulcius Felix??

Pistrinum e bottega di sex patulcius Felix

Pistrinum e bottega di sex patulcius Felix

Pistrinum e bottega di sex patulcius Felix

Casa del rilievo di telefo

Casa del rilievo di telefo

Casa del rilievo di telefo

Casa del rilievo di telefo

Casa del rilievo di telefo

Square at the house of the mayor.

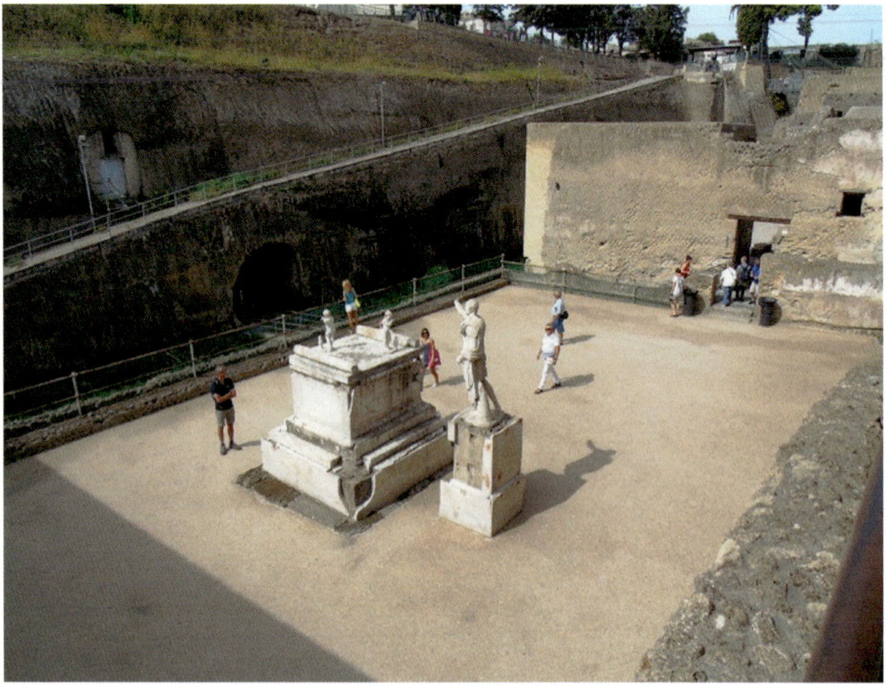

Area sacra. The holy place.

Area sacra. The holy place.

Square at the house of the mayor.

A view to the bridge at the entrance of the city.

Vault with victims of the disaster.

Some of the victims of the disaster.

Some of the victims of the disaster.

At the street Decumano Inferiore

Decumano Inferiore

Decumano Inferiore

Taberna vasaria, Pottery.

Taberna vasaria, Pottery.

Taberna vasaria

Again near the entrance at the street Cardo III Inferiore.

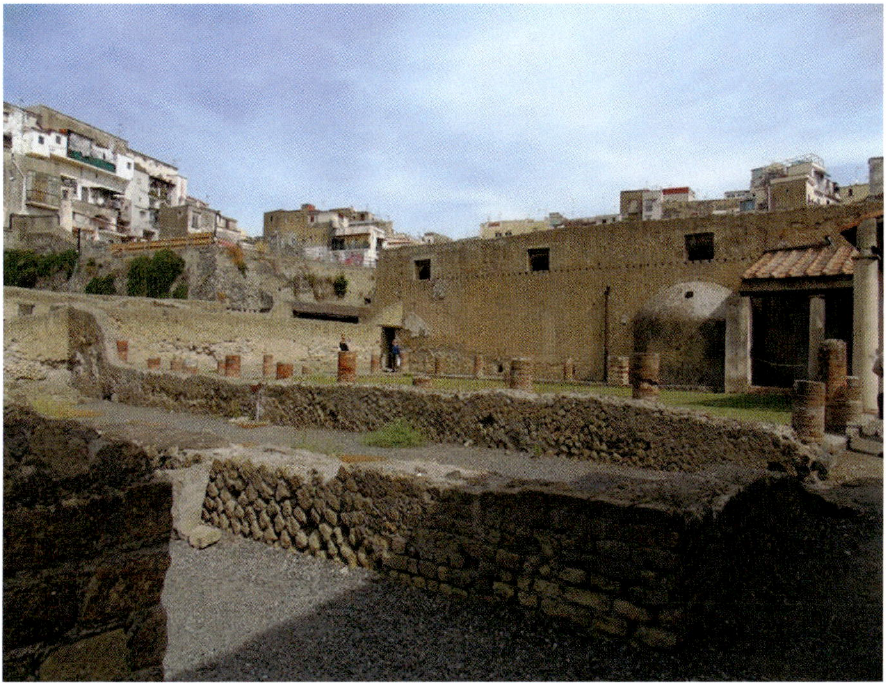

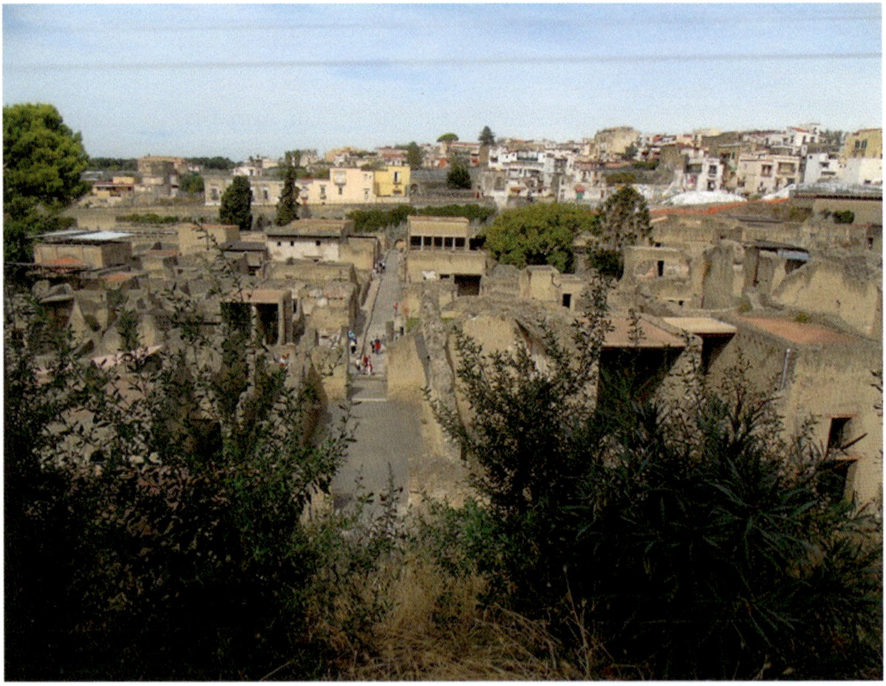

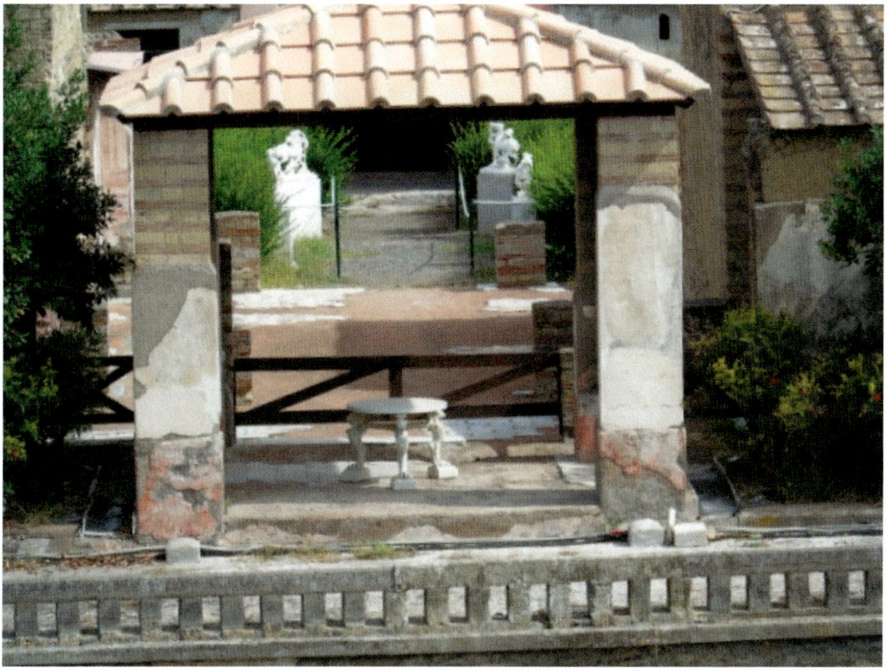

A last look at a bygone era.

Other books from the author:

Peter Klewa Ramazani

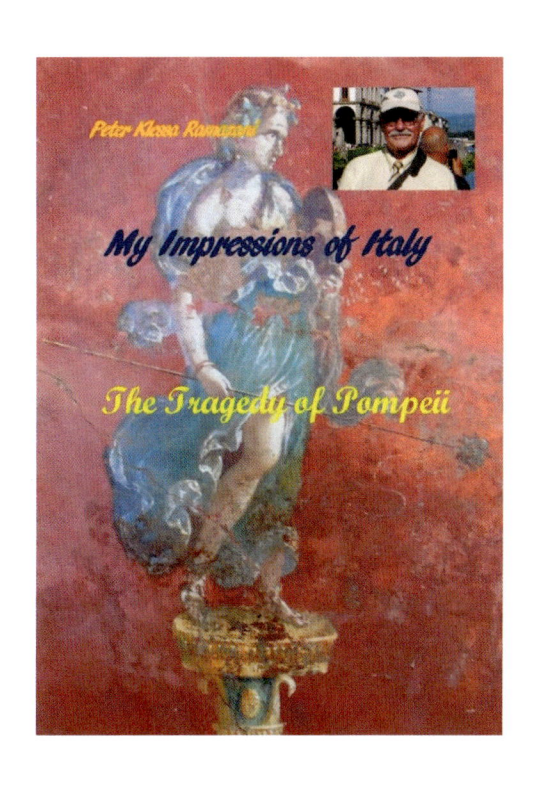

My Impressions of Italy

The Tragedy of Pompeii

Peter Klessa Ramazani

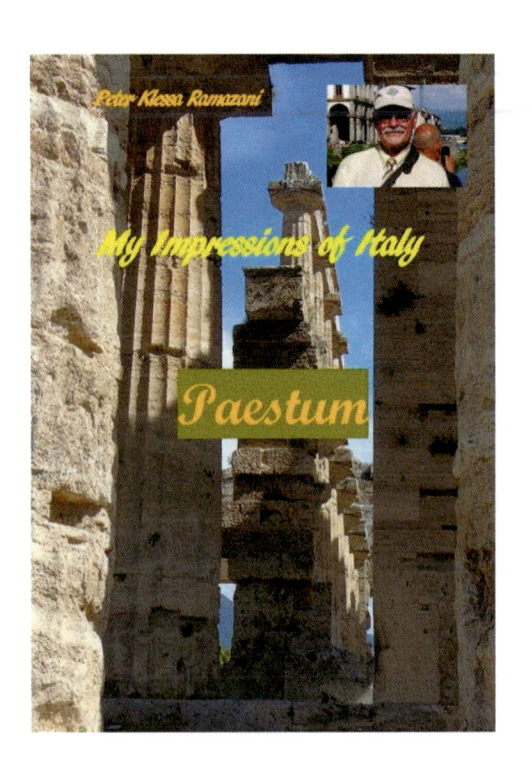

My Impressions of Italy

Paestum

Peter Klessa Ramazani

Printed in Great Britain
by Amazon